"Ivan Chow has a gift for celebrating archand through the most captivating origir
from Istanbul, Chow demonstrates his v
imagery unlike anything I can remember
is a beautiful work of art, cheerfully comp⌣.....ಒ ೩ಡ ॥ ಜಜಜಜ॥ಒ೫ in everyone's home."

- JAMES P. CRAMER, *founder, DesignIntelligence & Design Futures Council,
CEO (ret) American Institute of Architects, Washington, DC*

"The technological culture distances us forcefully from the direct encounter with reality. The act of drawing strengthens our sense of what is real. It is an irreplaceable way of structuring and understanding, recording and expressing perceptions.. Yet, sketches are not mere visual replicas of what has been observed. They fuse and convey the entire lived sensory experience, our being in the "flesh of the world", to quote Maurice Merleau-Ponty. Ivan Chow´s sketches mediate a sense of life, especially through the slight intentional displacement of line and color. We sense the temperature, hear the sounds, and smell the odours of Istanbul in these sketches."

- JUHANI PALLASMAA, *SAFA, HonFAIA, IntFRIBA; Professor emeritus;
Academician, International Academy of Architecture, Helsinki, Finland*

"Chow's *Travel Sketching* takes us on a geographical and artistic journey to Istanbul. Although the sketch lessons presented can apply to any travel experience, the richness of Istanbul is evident in every illustration and makes this immensely enjoyable. I particularly appreciate his honest accounts depicting challenges and workarounds of traveling as an artist touring with other people who are not sketching. We see the evolution of his sketch style, which is fascinating and encouraging. Travel Sketching inspires me to pull out my own sketchbooks and to list this book as required reading for my architecture students."

- ELAINE GALLAGHER ADAMS, AIA, *professor,
Savannah College of Art and Design, Savannah, Georgia*

"This is an ideal book to read and learn about travel sketching; its well laid out drawings and texts provide valuable and personal insights into how one may plan and enjoy the places and encounters on our travels. The different modes are exquisitely explained using Istanbul as a site. It is also in step with the times, explaining how digital images and formats like Facebook may be used to assist the craft."

- LAI CHEE KIEN, *architectural and urban historian
Singapore*

"The wait is over! Get your hands on this genre-bending book -- part travelogue, part how-to, and a wholly immersive experience for aspiring and professional traveler sketchers alike. Ivan's sketches represent a cross-section of iconic and ordinary Istanbul scenes. They are painted from his perch in a Burger King, on a myriad of pavements, on the stoop of a carpet shop, and everywhere in between. Readers will witness the author's agility and full breadth of artful re-creations of dozens of Turkish panoramas. His sketches make you feel as if you're a character in a scene – drawing you so close you can taste the plentiful morning kahvalti, smell the salty sea breeze amidst the rhythmic bobbing of the fishermens' poles from Galata Bridge, and seemingly sipping your Turkish çay in Taksim Squre with Ivan seated beside you – as a talented and approachable guide to travel sketching."

- ANGIE PLITCH, *Strategic Planning Director, Nike,*
Portland, Oregon

"A passionate educator and artist, Ivan Chow explores the rewarding pleasures of travel sketching through personal experiences and insightful tips that will benefit artists of any skill level. By engaging in the creative and intellectual exercise of sketching, he encourages us to adjust our reliance on selfie-sticks and smart phones by slowing down and fully engaging with the nuance and beauty of the places we visit."

- JUSTIN GUNTHER, *director, Fallingwater*
Mill Run, Pennsylvania

"Ivan shares his personal method of meditation and embodied thinking through his delightful and timeless sketches. This book will inspire you to stretch out your favorite travel moments in alternative ways other than quickly storing on social platforms."

- ENY LEE PARKER, *founder, Eny Lee Parker LLC*
Best New Emerging Designer at ICFF 2018, New York, New York

"This is a beautifully presented book which describes both the delights and practicalities of urban sketching. Ivan focuses on all aspects of drawing and painting on location, with gorgeous sketches to illustrate his creative journey around Istanbul. I particularly like how the book talks about the very human experience of what we do as artists working outside, and the issues of time, location and materials, which together make the activity so challenging but rewarding. A great read and a great insight into the wonderful world of what we do."

- IAN FENNELLY, *Hoylake, United Kingdom*

"Take a soulful walk through the streets of Istanbul and share in the inner dialogue of architect-artist Ivan Chow as the magical story of *Travel Sketching* unfolds with each page. Rich with insights on the technique, terminology and practice of travel sketching, this city walk celebrates the artfulness of architecture – its structures, materials and textures – as a framework for how we live. Each sketch records the urban experience with a personality of line and color, accompanied by a clarity and poetry of word and metaphor that captures a moment in time and revels in its lasting memory."

- JOHN MATTEO, *PE, FAAR, principal, 1200 Architectural Engineers, Alexandria, Virginia and lecturer, Johns Hopkins University, Baltimore, Maryland*

"Ivan's keen insights and clever tips on hand sketching are brilliantly displayed and well articulated in this delightful memoir of this travels to Istanbul. Creatively presented, even the novice will learn precise strategies for capturing the essence of a place in just a quick sketch. One will find practical advice on drawing tools as well as lessons learned about how best to capture a moment in time on your journey. There is truly no more personal way of expressing one's impression of a place than with travel sketching and, as you will discover in these pages, there is no one more talented than Ivan Chow."

- TIMOTHY MANSFIELD, *principal, Cambridge Seven Cambridge, Massachusetts*

"I don't know who first said "to draw is to see" but it is certainly the mantra of every travel sketcher and Ivan Chow definitely walks the walk in that arena. As the former leader of a study abroad program and longtime instructor of a travel sketching course in that program I have joyfully introduced more than 200 young designers to the art of travel sketching. For those who experience the aha moment, their way of seeing the world around them is changed forever. If this book was available when I was teaching it most certainly would have been required reading for my students."

- SEAN STEWART, *AIA, NCIDQ, former department chair, Wentworth Institute of Technology, Boston, Massachusetts*

"Travel Sketching is a wonderful primer on one man's journey through not only the capitol city of Turkey, but also through the processes and techniques in creating wonderful artwork. Throughout the book, Ivan demonstrates a wide-variety of quick sketch techniques that really draw out a sense of place and atmosphere of different settings. This book will serve as a tremendous supplement in the classroom and design studio and become a go-to for many artists and architects."

- ANDREW PAYNE, *dean, College of Architecture and Construction Management, Kennesaw State University, Kennesaw, Georgia*

Travel Sketching

DRAWING INSIGHTS FROM ISTANBUL

IVAN CHOW

TRAVEL SKETCHING:
DRAWING INSIGHTS FROM ISTANBUL
Copyright© 2020 by Ivan Chow.

All rights reserved. No part of this publication may be reproduced, distributed, or transmitted in any form or by any means, including photocopying, recording, or other electronic or mechanical methods, without the prior written permission of the author, except in the case of noncommercial uses permitted by copyright law. For permission requests, contact the author at ischow57@gmail.com.

ISBN: 978-1-63625-409-8
Library of Congress Control Number: 2020916267

Book design and illustrations by Ivan Chow © 2020

First edition published 2020
Printed in the United States of America

Dedicated to David Chow, who has encouraged me to publish my sketches for the better part of the past decade. Here you go, Dad.

ABOUT THE AUTHOR

Ivan Chow was born in England, grew up in Southeast Asia, and has worked in the United States and around the world as an architect, manager, educator and artist for almost four decades. He has practiced in design firms of various sizes; managed a private real estate investment company; worked in academia as a department chair and dean; and served as artist-in-residence at Frank Lloyd Wright's Fallingwater. Ivan has degrees in architecture from Harvard and Berkeley and a degree in theological studies from Gordon Conwell. He has three grown children, and currently lives with his wife in Savannah, Georgia.

Facebook @ivanchowsketches
Instagram @qkkdraw.

CONTENTS

TRAVEL SKETCHING 1

PLEIN AIR SKETCHING 7

PLEIN AIR PLUS 25

THE TRAVEL STUDIO 31

THE TRAVEL ART JOURNAL 41

AT THE END OF THE DAY 61

PREFACE

Travel sketching, an ancestor of sorts to Instagram, has changed the way I observe the world. I have discovered that the act and art of converting visual observation into graphic representation has far surpassed the benefits afforded by digital photography. What I have learned and enjoyed from the practice of travel sketching has enriched my travel experiences as well as deepened my appreciation of different cultures and peoples.

Although I have completed hundreds of travel sketches from all over the world, this book features only sketches I made from trips to and around Istanbul, Turkey, from 2015 to 2018 while my daughter was based there. These sketches from Istanbul represent the full range of sketching modes that I discuss within these pages and serve as good illustrations for the lessons learned and insights gleaned along the way. As a case study, they also aid in understanding the relationship between the act of drawing and the retention of the travel experience.

After having sketched under varying circumstances in many different locations, I have narrowed down this sub-genre of artistic expression into four general modes: plein air, plein air plus, travel studio, and travel art journaling. Each carries its own advantages and limitations, yet I have found that all are worthwhile endeavors. Though not an exhaustive list by any stretch of the imagination, they represent enough of a range of possibilities to keep any travel artist fully engaged while exploring the world.

Ivan Chow
Savannah, Georgia

TRAVEL SKETCHING

*W*hat is travel sketching? At its most basic level, it is simply the act of making a drawing while traveling. At a somewhat elevated level, it might be described as the practice of drawing observations and impressions experienced while on a journey. Probably at its most sophisticated level, travel sketching might be seen as the deliberate and planned undertaking of artistically recording observations, activities and sentiments as an integral and intentional part of the travel experience. Travel sketching is likely being practiced and enjoyed by millions of people around the world at every level.

According to Merriam-Webster, a sketch is "a rough drawing of something usually done as an initial draft…in contrast to a finished drawing, the word 'sketch' suggests imperfection and a lack of refinement." This is an important distinction to keep in mind when you are on-the-move away from home and will help prioritize what and when you set about to sketch a scene or situation. Travel sketches are rarely 100% accurate or representational. They are not necessarily intended to mimic real life but to capture impressions and unique experiences as a sort of visual journal.

Travel sketches can be

as simple as a detail of a building or piece of furniture, or as elaborate as a panoramic view of a city's skyline. They can be vignettes of unique flora, an interaction between fauna, or of people in unusual settings. However, travel sketches are almost always constrained by one encumbrance or another. This is especially true of plein air (in the open air) sketches, which are often affected by time, weather conditions, "field" conditions, and a host of other possible factors, both external and internal.

While the touch of an iPhone's camera button is convenient and efficient, sketching can afford much more in the way of enrichment and insight. Sketching slows down the experience of a place or object and forces the observer to pay closer attention to that which he or she might have traveled thousands of miles to see or experience.

During my trips to Istanbul, I completed as many of my sketches plein air as those that were completed in more comfortable settings like in a café or hotel room. Whenever plein air completion was in jeopardy, I would take a photo of the scene or object from the same vantage point to use for reference later on. Completing the sketch later also allowed me to add notation or commentary to further memorialize the experience.

What travel sketching is *not* is precision-driven rendering, realistic painting, or portraiture. While some sketches may end up being "frameable," most will live within the pages of a sketchbook or travel

This scene was sketched while standing at a street corner in Ortaköy, a lovely, waterfront mixed-used district along the Bosphorus. Due to pedestrian traffic, I only lasted about twenty minutes in that standing position before retreating to a nearby bench to finish watercoloring.

journal as part of a lifelong archive. People and animals don't have to look like they do in real life; along with trees and plants, they can show up as muddled shapes that lend themselves to the foreground or to provide context.

Both these sketches were completed plein air while sitting on one of the many tree-sheltered wrought iron benches populating the plaza, watching the boats docking and listening to a muezzin's call to prayer waft from the minarets. I decided to include just a couple of the many people criss-crossing the square to provide scale and took reference photos of the boats in the event they moved out of frame.

People arise early in Istanbul, quickly filling the streets with a haphazard but strangely workable throng of pedestrian, bicycular and vehicular traffic while stores regurgitated produce and wares onto makeshift display assemblies. Both corner store sketches were started plein air and completed later in the cafe (at right), where we enjoyed kahvalti, the traditional Turkish breakfast event.

Notice that little attention is paid to keeping lines straight or maintaining any real sense of accuracy. This sketch might have taken all of twenty minutes but captured the tight quarters that proprietors and patrons were clearly accustomed to.

This breathtaking view is from Ulus Park looking down at the beautiful Bosphorus Strait and the undulating array of buildings and boats that line its shores. I only had about thirty minutes for this sketch, which necessitated loose, squiggly, line work and quick dabs of Payne's Gray to establish shade and shadow patterns. Note that I drew a plant with individual leaves in the foreground to add depth of field.

One of the most hurried sketches I attempted was this vignette of apartment buildings cascading down a hillside and visually 'crashing' into a row of retail shops facing the Bosphorus between Ortaköy and Arnavutköy. A fifteen-minute blitz of lines and watercolor splotches with no thought about precision or accuracy.

PLEIN AIR SKETCHING

*W*hile travel sketching in plein air mode, I have tried a variety of postures and positions, depending on the setting. Most often I look for a bench (ideal but rare), stump, or rock to sit on. This allows me to place my sketchbook on my lap with a watercolor travel kit balanced on my left hand while drawing and painting with my right hand. However, there have been many occasions where I have chosen to stand. This offers two benefits: 1) having the choice of any viewpoint, and 2) intentionally limiting the time available to complete a sketch. The latter, while seemingly restrictive, has forced me into generating some of the most delightful sketches in my collection. I rarely sit on the ground to sketch, partly due to unknown or unsavory ground conditions and partly due to the ensuing backache after twenty to thirty minutes of intense sketching.

I have developed a quick sketching style that enables me to capture scenes and scenarios under fairly tight time constraints. I often use a multimedia tool combination of 0.2-0.4 mm fine line ink pens, a watercolor travel kit with travel brushes, and a landscape format 300 gsm cold-pressed watercolor

7

sketchbook. Additionally, I rarely leave home without extra loose watercolor paper, a few drawing pencils, and a watercolor reservoir brush.

Frequently without the luxury of a horizontal surface on which to place separate painting tools, I have defaulted to a carry-all field kit made by Winsor & Newton (professional line) that comprises a set of twelve half-pans, fold-out palette leaves, a removable palette-cum-water reservoir, and a clip-on water well; all of which can be carried in one hand. That leaves me free to move about and sketch on-the-fly, so to speak. Plein air travel sketching is not a tidy business but a rough-edged, often frenzied, invigorating exercise in focused observation and rapid-fire drawing and painting. This is also why I always bring along a wad of napkins or paper towels. Travel sketching involves spills, drips, uncontrollable washes, and a constant need to dab away excess fluids from brushes, paper, and myself!

In general, my plein air sketches reside in an A5 size landscape format watercolor sketchbook (about 5.5" x 8.5"), of which there are countless varieties. My favorites have been those with an elastic closure strap and a back pocket. The former helps keep pages flat whereas the latter is useful for supporting documents such as torn excerpts from a brochure or a test strips of watercolor paper. While every page can be used, in some sketchbooks only one side of each sheet is textured which generally receives watercolor better than the other. Also, if you think your sketches might one day be framed, avoiding sketching on the back side allows the page to be torn off and matted.

The choice of a subject to sketch is a delightfully personal exercise. While photo ops from designated vista points might dictate a more typified viewpoint, sketching allows the freedom to curate the view. I have found myself "framing" a sketch from behind overhanging tree branches, through doorways or tunnels, and including interesting features in the foreground or distant background, whether or not they are actually in my frame of view. This is part of the joy of travel sketching—choosing what you want to remember about a place or an experience rather than worrying about executing an accurate representation of it.

In approaching each sketch, I have adopted what has become an informal

From where I was sitting, the large boat in the foreground actually obscured those in the background. I conveniently "pushed" it back to gain a wider field of vision.

but important ritual. The first step is to relax my mind, heart, and breathing. This can be achieved rather quickly, often with a few deep breaths and intentionally opening your mind to the immediate environment—the sounds, the smells, the feel of the wind on your face, and the quality of the light being cast.

    The second step is to survey the context within which the object of the sketch will live. Study the ground plane below, the sky or tree canopy above, and the adjacencies on either side. I may not sketch all or any of these elements, but I thoroughly enjoy this step of the ritual - soaking up the ambiance of the immediate surroundings. I often remind myself that I am visiting this place to experience something different, to see things I haven't seen before, and to open my mind to the unusual and the invigorating.

This panoramic sketch spread across two pages of my sketchbook in order to capture the Ortaköy waterfront facing the expanse of the Bosphorus, with boats and the sweep of the coastline in the background. On the right is the elegant House Hotel developed from a 19th century Ottoman residence. I had over an hour for this sketch and invested quite a bit of time lightly laying out the buildings and background in pencil before committing to the ink work. Note how I handled light and shadow, as simply as possible, keeping only the surfaces facing the river in the light and throwing everything else in shade.

The third step is, to me, one of the greatest returns-on-investment of travel sketching. Once I start the sketch, I find that my mind begins focusing on that singular task, and everything else— random thoughts in my head, stresses of trip logistics, mental baggage I brought along from work—gradually fades away. For a relatively untroubled twenty to thirty minutes, my mind experiences reprieve. This is where it is important to realize that it is as much the process as it is the product that makes travel sketching so enjoyable.

Once that ritual is over, where and how do I start a sketch? Left-to-right? Top-down? Outside-in? Because of my background as an architect, I typically choose to draw buildings and features within the built environment. As such, I almost always start with lightly constructing and outlining the building, plaza, streetscape, or garden. Because we live in a three-dimensional world, everything we have seen since the day we were born is viewed in perspective. Almost everything you draw will involve, to a lesser or greater degree, a basic understanding of perspective. While learning how to draw in perspective is a lifelong pursuit, here are four "always" principles to keep in mind when constructing a scene:

- All parallel lines always converge to a vanishing point.
- Vanishing points are always on the horizon line.
- The horizon line is always at the eye of the observer.
- Objects closer are always larger than objects further away.

When drawing a building, all parallel lines along the front façade will angle down or up in such a way as to meet at a single point along a horizontal line at your eye level. All parallel lines that are perpendicular to the front façade will angle down or up to meet at another point along the same horizon line but typically on the opposite side of the first vanishing point. Some vanishing points can be very far away, literally off the page, so this is where you have to use your imagination to approximate where these parallel lines converge. Once you have determined the vanishing points, all objects and

This summertime sketch of the renowned Taksim Square was completed in one sitting but from multiple positions. I had begun sketching seated on the pavement in front of the Taksim Mosque facing the square. Within 10 minutes, the local constabulary approached, ordering me to move. The sketch continued while standing about fifty feet to one side, which required walking to and from my original position for reference, and back to the "safe zone" to continue sketching, clutching my watercolor kit and sketchbook in one hand, pages flapping in the breeze; brush in the other hand, pinky finger trying to hold down the page. I ended up crossing the street into the square proper and finishing the forty-five minute sketch seated on a low rail around the Republic Monument. Even under these conditions, I was pleased by how the sketch reflected the windy conditions, the movement of people and the "life" of this symbolic gathering place.

features in your sketch, once conformed to these perspective guidelines, should look "right."

Completion, not unlike beauty, is in the eye of the beholder. That is to say, there is no point at which you must or should stop sketching. Many factors will undoubtedly contribute to interruptions and change of plans. Antsy travel companions, changing weather conditions, or the bus that parks right in front of you obstructing your view may impede the satisfactory completion of a sketch. Nevertheless, I always try to plan a sketch according to the time I think might be available. Whether it be fifteen minutes while waiting for gathering family members or a multi-hour block of dedicated sketch time, I find it useful to plan ahead. This helps determine the scope, speed, and style of a sketch.

For short periods, I will only do a vignette (a small portion of a scene) with

one or two interesting features, maybe only occupying a portion of a page. For these quick impressions, I usually adopt a very loose, light-handed style involving squiggly-line ink work and simple washes with a few color accents or hints of shade and shadow. If I have the luxury of an uninterrupted hour, I will be more ambitious and attempt a panoramic view across two pages of my sketchbook using tighter, more precise line work and a broader color palette.

This quick sketch completed during the winter, two years after the one above, was from the shelter of an adjacent second floor Burger King restaurant. It's quite different in "feel."

What often happens

despite the planning and style adjustments is that I end up only partway through a sketch, just (or way) short of my intended goal, when I realize I've got to pack up and leave my prized spot. Disappointment and that irksome sense of incompletion start forming in the back of my mind (or sometimes in the pit of my stomach). That's when I tell myself, don't sweat it. Before I leave, I'll take a photo of what I was sketching from the same viewpoint as this will come in handy when I have time to finish the sketch later on.

This view of the Blue Mosque in Eminönü was sketched from the front stoop of a carpet shop along a tiny street in the south corner. I secured permission using mime and a fair amount of head-nodding, and in exchange, the proprietors took multiple selfies and brought me lots of tea.

We had breakfast at this quaint restaurant in Arnavutköy that I wanted very much to sketch. But right outside and obstructing the view was the owner's bright red sports car. It was easy enough to "move" the car slightly off-frame to capture the desired scope but leaving enough of it in to enrich this memory.

This really enjoyable sketch was made while standing on the Galata Bridge that spans the Golden Horn between Karaköy and Eminönü, watching the omnipresent fishermen working their surf rods in the persistent hunt for sardines and horse mackerel. This longstanding tradition involves the dangling of shiny lures or baited hooks into the water and bobbing the rods to attract fish, like a never-ending dance. What the sketch couldn't convey were the smells of cut bait, the sounds of passing traffic and the chill of the salty breeze. But looking at this sketch brings them all back to mind.

Beşiktaş Square, along the busy thoroughfare between Ortaköy and Karaköy, is a popular local hot spot, centered on a boisterous fish market surrounded by a dense maze of shops, restaurants and bars. Across the main road is a transportation hub with a ferry terminal, bus depot and taxi stand bordered to the north by a multi-story, multi-restaurant, building overlooking the terminal and the Bosphorus. On a cold day in December 2017, after a invigorating ferry ride along the shoreline, I found a table on the topmost floor of the restaurant building with a great view of the Square. The sketch took over an hour, interrupted only by waitstaff bringing me hot tea refills and asking me unintelligible questions in Turkish. As I was leaving, one of the waiters approached me with a
request, which I deciphered from a spattering of English words and many hand gestures to be: would I sketch their building for the owner? Unprepared for the request and out of time, I left with no response except to take a photo of the building as seen from the ferry terminal. Back in my 'travel studio,' I worked up the sketch (on the left), returned to the restaurant a few days later, and presented it to a random waiter with the most rudimentary instructions. Hopefully it made to the owner.

There can really be no trip to Istanbul that misses out on a visit to the legendary Ayasofya (a.k.a. Hagia Sofia). This hulking historic mosque built over centuries presents itself not so much as a work of architecture as a reflection of cultural evolution. Its sheer mass and presence commands silent attention and, of course, the obligatory photo ops. For a sketch artist, however, the Ayasofya presents endless opportunities.

The first sketch (across top) was started on site, but completed later that same day in travel studio. The second (across bottom) was done plein air but in two sittings, one before and the other after our tour of the interior. (My travel companions wouldn't wait!) The third very quick sketch (top) was completed two years later from one of the park benches facing the north facade. During that third sketch, other tourists asked to take photos of me while I worked. There was even a selfie request by two new 'fans' with whom I was able to share my online portfolio. This has become a regular occurrence, which adds to the enjoyment of travel sketching. It is worth pointing out the noticeable difference between the relative 'tightness' of the 2015 sketches and the 'looseness' of the 2017 version. This I attribute to the on-going internal battle between the precision and accuracy required of and by the trained architect in me and the "freedom of expression" sought by my inner artist.

Lessons re-learned

- *Adding shade and shadow is critical in conveying form and depth*

- *Even just suggestions of people are so important in establishing scale*

- *Looser line work and hints of color sometimes convey the 'spirit' of a place better than precision or accuracy might*

These interior sketches were made while standing within the cavernous expanse of this 1,500 year-old Byzantine monument to Ottoman architecture and culture. The contrast from the warmth and bustle of the exterior to the hushed coolness of the inside almost mandated reverence. This is where that Winsor & Newton professional watercolor travel kit came in handy, albeit restrictive. Being able to clutch both watercolor kit and sketchbook in one hand is a cultivated skill and immensely useful for situations like this. It was important to limit the scope of the sketches knowing that I would likely not be able to stand-in-place for much longer than twenty minutes at a time.

Another observation is that the longer I spent sketching, the less patience I had with subsequent sketches. As such, the ones completed later would either be looser with more 'spirit,' or hopelessly unpresentable. One example was a seven-minute vignette completed while waiting on family during a restroom break.

I realized early in each sketch that I wouldn't have time to capture the ubiquitous and exquisite details that populated the interior spaces. Instead - and this has become usual practice - I used loose and squiggly lines within the detailed elements to imply the presence and 'texture' of said detail. The density and thickness of line work should be commensurate with the amount of detail within that element. Both sketches on this page illustrate this point, especially along the borders above the arches and on the soffits of the arches themselves. Even exquisite Corinthian column capitals can be represented with small groupings of random squiggles.

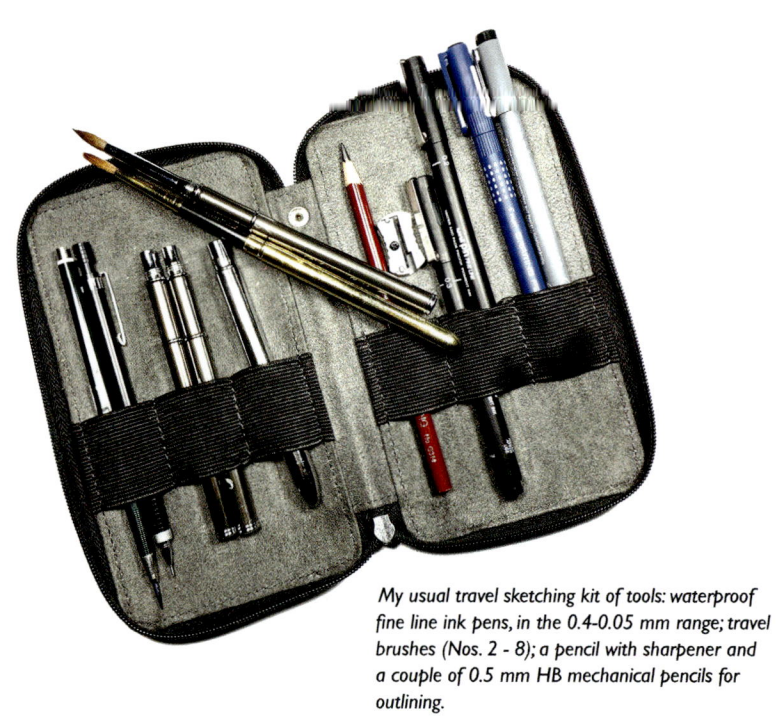

My usual travel sketching kit of tools: waterproof fine line ink pens, in the 0.4-0.05 mm range; travel brushes (Nos. 2 - 8); a pencil with sharpener and a couple of 0.5 mm HB mechanical pencils for outlining.

PLEIN AIR PLUS

Some of the most satisfying evenings I have spent in hotels when traveling have been occupied with completing unfinished plein air sketches. While the visual experience is still fresh in mind, not much of the spirit of the sketch is lost when completion is slightly delayed. I emphasize "slightly" because it is often too tempting to leave an unfinished sketch until I return home. Trust me when I say it'll never get done. It pays off in spades to finish the sketch while you are still on the road.

One night, we decided to cross the Bosphorus to visit a night market on the Asian side of Istanbul. While waiting for the ferry to depart, I began this night sketch but quickly realized that side-to-side wave action of a moored vessel was not particularly conducive to line work. So I took a photo, pocketed my sketchbook and spent the rest of the evening soaking up the ambiance of Turkish nightlife. The sketch was finished the next morning at breakfast with the memory of the evening before still fresh in mind.

This is one of my favorite travel sketches. We were taking a much-needed break under the shade of the colonnade at Topkapi Palace, and this view of the structural complexity of cascading domes and the elegant way they met the pointed arches below was quite irresistable. I bargined for time and was able to get the line work done and most of the color applied before having to leave. It only took a few minutes of shade and shadow touch up later that day to complete the drawing. Quite fun!

There are two reasons for this exhortation. First, it allows you to claim that what you produced was indeed a travel sketch, not an after-I-came-home sketch. The second reason for completing the sketch soon afterward is to take advantage of the muscle memory that is likely still embedded just below the surface of your mind and in your hand and fingers, allowing you to continue the style and pace of the sketch you began just a few hours earlier with some measure of consistency.

This last concept of muscle memory is

an intriguing one when it comes to travel sketching. Unlike studio painting or portraiture, travel sketching depends on rapid-fire synaptic connections between your brain and hand as the former processes visual and cognitive observation that the latter has to represent in a relatively short period of time. This brain-to-hand relationship is not easily recognized let alone understood, but in my experience, has a direct bearing on the outcome of a sketch.

For example, in sketching a street scene bustling with activity and sound, my brain needs to will my hand to guide the pen or pencil in such a way as to freeze or suspend a moment in time. To accomplish that, my brain must choose one out of a broad and fluid range of moments, convey a snapshot of that moment to my hand, which proceeds as quickly as possible to put those impressions down

Another must-see in Istanbul is the Grand Bazaar, a cultural and commercial labyrinth that nestles like an irregularly coiled serpent on a hillside just below the Istanbul University in the district of Eminönü. This plein air plus sketch began comfortably at a cafe table, but was rudely interrupted by harried travel companions and a proprietor frowning disapproval at my not having ordered a cup of ubiquitous Turkish çay.

on paper, even as those moments pass and vanish. This dynamic back-and-forth between brain and hand goes into high gear during a plein air sketch, creating a surge of drawing momentum towards the completion of that sketch.

In his book *The Thinking Hand*, Finnish architect Juhani Pallasmaa theorizes about the symbiotic relationship between the mind and the hand. In parsing the act of drawing, Pallasmaa writes, "In fact, every act of sketching and drawing produces three different sets of images: the drawing that appears on the paper, the visual image recorded in my cerebral memory, and the muscular memory of the act of drawing itself." I have found this to be quite true when putting off the completion of a sketch too long; my hand (used here to include my fingers) tends to "forget" the rhythm of what I began drawing, requiring either an uninspired restart or total abandonment.

In general, I find that completing a sketch within a few hours is optimal, with almost no loss of recall or motivation. In fact, many of my sketches have turned out better with the benefit of a more comfortable position of body and hand, and less stressful conditions within which to work. When I can have my sketchbook, watercolor kit, and instruments on a flat surface, I gain more control over line drawing and brushwork. Some of the spirit of a sketch may be lost as I tend to tighten up when the pressure's off, but not so much as to change its outcome significantly.

This is one of those paradoxical phenomena: I become more stressed when drawing plein air fast and loose than when I take the time to slow down in a more comfortable environment, but my sketches often feel more alive under the former conditions. Further adding complexity

to this irony is that I enjoy the latter conditions more than the former. Once in a long while, I will find myself having the best of both worlds—drawing plein air in relatively comfortable conditions such as the coziness of a café which turns itself into a remote "travel studio."

I didn't particularly like the way these sketches turned out but they serve as an important lesson if sketching is attempted while on a guided tour such as the one we embarked on at Yıldız Chalet behind the palace in Yıldız Park. As the tour guide recited talking points, I stepped aside from the group and began the line work of the oval stairwell with the wood railing. I was less than half way through when the guide moved the group to the next room. I took a quick photo of the stairwell and joined the group, starting a new sketch of the ornate hallway (above right). Same thing happened when we moved to the main entrance atrium, where I began the third interior sketch of the main stairway. None of the sketches were close to being complete when the tour ended. But with photos in hand and a low wall to sit on outside, I was able to complete the line work, add color and sketched the exterior view (above top) in less than an hour. Lesson learned: there is too much stress involved in sketching during a guided tour!

One of my favorite travel studio set-ups!

THE TRAVEL STUDIO

*A*nother mode of travel sketching, while somewhat less exciting or stimulating though no less rewarding, is what I call travel-studio sketching. In this mode, you create a temporary and makeshift artist "studio" wherever you might be. The setup and equipment are virtually the same as for plein air sketching, except that the work is done in the relative comfort of a café or hotel room where

Ferry dock at town of
Küçüksu on the
Bosphorus, 2017.

time and the elements are not as much of a factor in the production of a sketch. While I thoroughly enjoy plein air sketching, I must admit that travel-studio sketching has afforded me some of the most satisfying sketches in my portfolio.

A travel studio comprises all the artist tools mentioned above with the addition of a flat surface on which to draw, a place to sit comfortably for a couple of hours, and most importantly, a digital record or clear mental picture of the object or scene you wish to sketch. This works exceedingly well when traveling with companions when there is no time to break away or linger. The same astute

Küçüksu waterway cafes.

32

observation and discernment are required to select what you will sketch later, but only a minute or two is required for a quick visual survey and to take a few photos from different vantage points. In addition to taking photos framing the view that I intend to sketch, I have found it helpful to take close-up photos of some key features within the composition. This helps back in the "studio" when you are wondering how to draw elements that might have been hidden in shadow or partially obscured by people or vehicles.

The intricacy of fenestration on this archway caught my attention on a long walk between Karaköy and Beşiktaş. But with no place to position myself on a busy sidewalk along a highway with bumper-to-bumper traffic, this was a perfect candidate for a travel studio sketch.

In my travels, I have created studio environments in many different settings. Anything and everything has served as a temporary studio space, from part of

the dining table at an Airbnb or a host's apartment; to a hotel room or at the bar in the lobby; along counters next to airline gates while in transit; in quiet cafes and noisy restaurants; and even in public libraries. What I find counts toward a successful travel-studio sketching experience is not as much the physical setting as it is my state of mind while sketching—that same relaxed, focused, and sharply observant state that I might adopt during plein air sketching. The important thing, in my mind, is to complete the sketch during my travels, not after.

After many years of navigating the blurry intersections between plein air, plein air plus

A street in Istanbul

Istanbul rooftops

There is an iteration of travel-studio sketching that I will feel compelled to undertake from time to time, and that is vicarious travel sketching—sketches of experiences and locales that other people are going through in places I would unlikely visit. In those instances, I might be at home or on the road and receive a texted or emailed photo that is just too compelling to ignore. While not nearly as satisfying as plein air or travel-studio sketching, vicarious sketching has its moments. Both sketches on this page were photos from our daughter who was working in Istanbul at the time and looking for a place to stay. I'm not sure what propelled me to embark upon these vignettes except to somehow share my daughter's experience in absentia.

and travel-studio sketching, I have developed different mental approaches for each mode of sketching. In plein air and plein air plus modes, I mentally prepare myself for a fairly high level of (good) stress coupled with lower expectations in terms of output volume. My goal is to achieve some measure of quality within a realistic scope of work. In other words, I have to keep in mind what I can most likely accomplish within the time available.

In travel-studio sketching mode - which is generally when I know in advance that there will be no time for plein air sketching - I often find myself anticipating the future respite of "studio time" with secret delight. After a long stretch of hectic touring and exploring, sketching in travel studio brings perfect closure to the day.

Some of my most satisfying sketches have been the result of planning their execution intentionally with *both* plein air and travel-studio stages in mind. This requires some forethought to make sure my initial fieldwork on the sketch does not jeopardize its completion in studio. For example, I need not hurry the line work knowing I will complete it later; or need not attempt tricky sky washes while standing knowing I will have a flat surface on which to work with in studio.

In 2017, on my second trip to Istanbul in the middle of winter, I had the opportunity to take an inexpensive (and highly recommended) public ferry ride along the Bosphorus, beginning at Beşiktaş, heading north on the European side under the Sultan Mehmet Bridge to Arnavutköy and then back down to Küçüksu and Beylerbeyi along the Asian side. With on-and-off privileges at no additional cost, I was able to dedicate the better part of an afternoon to sketching some of the most romantic scenes along this historic waterway.

In some instances, such as at the Küçüksu Palace and Beylerbeyi Mosque, I was able to find great vantage points from which to sketch while seated. The scenes viewed while cruising along the Bosphorus, however, were more challenging. Even though the ferry had an enclosed passenger seating area, the best views were from the open deck, which at the time was uncomfortably chilly, especially for bare-hand sketching. I started a couple of outlines, but with the cold wind and unpredictable movement of the ferry, it fast became a losing battle.

Along the Bosphorus coast at Beylerbei, Istanbul Asia – DEZ 2017

Instead, I took a series of photos of each scene as we passed, keeping in mind that I would be sketching them later that day without the benefit of a revisit. The exercise then became one of closer observation of the character and feel of the small towns lining the shores of the river and how the buildings and public areas met the water. I noticed groups of people fishing along the shore with long surf poles; the ubiquitous use of red-tiled roofs on homes; and the towering minarets of mosques presenting their faces along the esplanade. I noticed the muddy character of the sky populated by a patchwork of cloud types, some more saturated with moisture than others. I felt the constant breeze that swept clean the waterfront streets and kept caps and scarves tightened around heads and necks. These observations, because they were made intentionally, would come back as fresh memories when I later completed them in travel-studio.

For this series of travel-studio sketches, I decided to go borderless, that is, images drawn and painted right to the edges of the paper. The tendency to maintain borders rather than go borderless on a drawing has plagued me for the better part of my career as an architect. My personal preference has always to either leave or design intentional borders around my drawings. Perhaps it comes from decades of compliance to the way design and construction drawings have been formatted with borders and title blocks. Whatever the reason, borders have become an integral - and to a large degree required - part of how I format a drawing. For me to go borderless required courage.

This is where a protected environment of travel-studio offers some huge benefits for travel sketching, with its ability to control washes and bleeds; to be able to blot and dab; and to achieve low-angle dry-brush strokes. The character of these sketches turned out far better than anticipated, and more closely reflected the delightful experience I had on the Bosphorus ferry ride that afternoon.

The final sketch of that day was of an evening scene from the top floor of a multi-story restaurant building overlooking the Beşiktaş ferry terminal at the sun setting behind the Bosphorus Bridge. It was a scene that I knew would not last long enough to be sketched plein air, as it would be a matter of minutes before

the sun disappeared below the horizon. Nevertheless, it was such a heartwarming scene - the confluence of the sunset, the unloading of the ferries, and the echoes of simit (bagel) vendors hawking their wares to bedraggled workers trudging their way across the platform - that it begged to be sketched later in studio as a sort of dessert to the main meal of the day's travel sketching.

THE TRAVEL ART JOURNAL

    One of the most invigorating formats for travel sketching is one I have recently become more intentional about, and which has been received with a great deal of enthusiasm, especially when posted on social media in audio-visual format. On platforms such as Facebook or Instagram, posts of photos or videos depicting scenes or people accompanied by descriptive captions are fairly typical ways of sharing travel experiences. Posting travel sketches, however, is quite unique and arguably more interesting. Adding written captions or commentary makes this approach of sharing travel experiences even richer and more memorable.

    Enter the travel art journal. While not necessarily a new genre or form of expression, it has become for me a fresh approach to sharing experiences in an otherwise digitally saturated world. A travel art journal has the potential to transform travel sketching into a unique mode of expression, combining drawing with handwriting and composition to create a new "voice." My forays into developing art journal sequences have been thoroughly rewarding, as I am able to combine my drawing skills with an interest in writing to communicate much more than either discipline can on its

own. That's probably why comic books and graphic novels have such appeal and why skillful cartooning can be so influential.

A travel art journal can be formatted in as many ways as there are personalities. My favorite format is an A5 size journal (about 5.5" x 8.5"), either in landscape or portrait mode, with sufficiently thick paper to stand up to waterproof ink lines and light washes (80 lb. minimum, 140 lb. preferred). As with sketchbooks, an elastic closure strap and inside back cover pocket can be helpful. In addition to the usual array of tools I might have on hand for travel sketching, I would add a few choice writing instruments, such as a chisel-nib fountain or calligraphy pen.

As the name implies, a *journal* is a regular log of activities and events that occur roughly in chronological order. A *travel journal* might memorialize the daily travel schedule, places visited, people met, cuisine enjoyed and souvenirs acquired. A *travel art journal* adds the element of artwork in the form of sketches, doodles, graphic illustrations, even glued-on collages using torn excerpts from brochures, tickets, receipts, and labels. I have found this last exercise quite a satisfying way of closing out a busy day of touring.

Travel art journal entries are unique compositional challenges. In its simplest form, each page might contain a few sketch vignettes describing the activities of the day. Arranging the sketches on the page may require some foresight, consideration of size, scope, and subject of each vignette and how they might tell the story of the day's experiences. Each entry becomes a graphic design exercise involving the layout of sketches, diagrams, titles and text.

The addition of handwritten text to a composition is both an enriching enhancement and a potentially stressful endeavor. It is enriching because it adds information, flavor, and specificity to a sketch. Potentially stressful because, unlike the editability afforded by computer software programs, each phrase or caption needs to be somewhat thought through and composed before being physically written within the space available or created.

I love to write by hand and am constantly experimenting with different writing instruments with different tips, nibs, and inks. It's almost an obsession with me, and I am easily disappointed when my writing falters. Having said that, I highly enjoy narrow, flat-nosed calligraphy pens for travel art journaling, especially used in a generally cursive lettering style. However, most fountain pen type of writing instruments with reservoirs have no tolerance for waterproof ink, which tends to clog the fins and feed tubes. This often leaves me with little choice but to use the waterproof ink felt-tipped pens I used to sketch with for lettering as well. A real calligraphic treat is to use Speedball dip nibs with bottled India ink, although both have not proven to travel well.

There are so many interesting ways to express yourself once in the

Suleymaniye mosque
Istanbul

groove of travel art journaling. The inclusion of people with speech and thought bubbles is a great way of adding interest and conveying sentiment. Self-portraits can show how you feel, sometimes better than words can describe. Self-portraits with thought bubbles offer an even better way to communicate your feelings. Often, I find my sketch vignettes growing and expanding on to the adjacent page, sometimes even falling off the page. Entries are frequently mood-driven, sometimes showing frustration or impatience by the haphazardness of the line work or sloppiness of coloring. Other times, the lettering is deliberate, and the sketches are precise, reflecting pensiveness or thoughtfulness.

    Regardless of how these entries have turned out, I have noticed a common thread weaving its way through all the sketching I do. Through having sketched certain elements many times before, my drawing hand has developed its own method and style of drawing trees, people, pavement, various building components

and even furniture - a sort of "pattern language" of its own. Often I find myself "zoning out" while sketching, especially after having constructed the overall view and distinguishing features, as my hand "thinks" on its own to finish the sketch. It's as though my drawing hand knows what to do without me consciously participating - that thinking hand!

On this and the following pages are the entries made during a family vacation to Istanbul and a side trip to Cappadocia in the winter of 2018. My previous trips had been either alone or with one other traveling companion. Now being "in tow" with a family of five, my travel sketching forays would be relatively limited, thereby necessitating a creative combination of plein air plus, travel-studio, and travel art journaling while enjoying sightseeing with my family.

With the company of family members who had never been to Istanbul, we re-toured the usual suspects within the city—the Ayasofya, Grand Bazaar, Galata

Tower, and Taksim Square—while enjoying local shopping, wet markets, and traditional Turkish breakfast. This gave me the chance to sketch different views and details of places I had visited before. Our side trip to Cappadocia was to the town of Göreme, where we stayed at the Kelebek (butterfly) Cave Hotel carved into the face of the hillside and surrounded by ancient volcanic rock formations known as Fairy Chimneys.

Into these unusually-shaped formations, people had once carved homes and churches out of the soft volcanic ash between and below more resilient layers of soil, creating a unique, largely hidden, and protected community nestled into the natural landscape. Probably the most memorable experience—besides finding a great Szechuan restaurant in town—was a crack-of-dawn, hot-air balloon ride that took us high above the region for some breathtaking scenery.

Watching balloon skins being filled with propane-fired flames while becoming dwarfed by the sheer immensity of the inflated behemoths and realizing that this is

how air travel occurred for well over a hundred years before the advent of airplanes afforded me a deeper appreciation of human innovation...and courage! Floating in freezing silence a mile above Cappadocia, propelled only by the atmospheric winds and surrounded by scores of other hot-air balloons, was truly surreal.

For me, making those daily entries into my travel art journal became one of the most enjoyable activities of that trip. Like a traveler's executive summary of sorts, each entry became an anticipated evening (and sometimes, morning) ritual. In addition to sketching memorable sights and sounds, the exercise also helped me think about and record interesting information or lessons learned from the day's experiences.

Another word about composition. As you can see from these travel art journal entries, sketches and text seem somewhat randomly thrown on the pages; this is only partially true. Since much of the work was done in travel-studio mode, I had time to consider graphic layout concurrent with deciding on the scope of

the sketches and written commentary.

The approach I took was to make the sketches first, then arrange the captions to fill in the available white space. I also used a mixture of drawings at different scales to create interest on a page, such as overall views of a building or space combined with details of interesting portions. Also, by allowing some vignettes to blend together, interesting page compositions evolved.

However, while the prescriptive method described above sounds straightforward enough, this is only half the story. Unrecognized by my conscious mind, there was another force at work. It is what Pallasmaa refers to as "embodied thinking," where parts of the body - in this case, the hand - have the ability to remember and to connect those memories in service of the mind's intent. In my mind, I wanted to compose a page of vignettes and captions that would summarize and express, on paper, the memorable experiences of the day. I knew in concept what I wanted to draw, but in reality, it wasn't until my hand started drawing that the composition began to take shape. And as it drew, new ideas, arrangements, spatial relationships began to develop based on what it had drawn before and what it knew my mind wanted to achieve.

Again Pallasmaa from *The Thinking Hand*: "A drawing is an image that compresses an entire process fusing a distinct duration into that image. A sketch is in fact a temporal image, a piece of cinematic action recorded as a graphic image." In fact, my hand, in service of my mind, was producing the equivalent of a video clip encapsulating the events of the day.

Take for example the art journal entry featuring the Fairy Chimneys in Göreme (next page). I remember starting one image at the left side of the page with only a general idea of what the next image was and where it would actually be placed. As the first vignette developed, the decision was made to place the second vignette at the top and running across the double page, leaving white space below possibly for captions. Similarly, the third image was drawn to fill the space at the bottom right corner. The thing is, I don't actually remember making these subsequent decisions!

Evidently supplementing that conscious prescriptive method was another creative force working through my "thinking hand" to compose, edit, embellish and produce the story on the page. It's a little like magic - where the outcome, while inexplicable, is surprising and delightful.

I mention all this in an attempt to explain why I have enjoyed travel sketching - and especially travel art journaling - so much. While I usually have a general idea what I'm trying to accomplish with each sketch or entry, I can rarely predict its outcome. Instead, I am learning to trust my hand and its embodied experience to use the appropriate skills in its résumé - line quality, drawing speed, scope, compositional balance and its developed "pattern language"- to achieve the ends which my mind had only imagined. In fact, there were times when my mind had to catch up with what my hand was doing. Therein lies what some might call "mistakes," where the disobedient, wayward, hand does something the mind did not intend for it to do. I call it travel sketching.

When I look back at these entries, I have two buckets of fond memories. One is filled with the experiences themselves; how interesting, enjoyable, tiring and educational they were. The other contains pearls of joy formed out of the precious time I spent sketching and make entries in my travel art journal.

We don't value craft the way it once was valued. Yet, this sort of overdoes it, which of course was the intent of the baroque style - to swing the pendulum to the other side of the Renaissance.

Construction began in 1843, opened in 1856.
Architects:
Garabet Balyan
Evanis Kalfa

Palace gate along Dolmabahçe Road, Istanbul.
Influences of baroque, neoclassical and Ottoman architecture.   21 Dec 2018

22 Dec 2018

← CAP (dark)
← STRIATIONS
← SHAFT
← BASE (dark)

On approach to Göreme, a forest of phallic rock formations greet unsuspecting visitors. Formed out of lava stream protrusions after the softer Cappadocian rock weathered away over millions of years.

Dwellings carved out of the natural Cappadocian rock mixed with new development using similar materials and color palette.

2 Feb. Arrived at 5 home in Cappadocia after a short 2 hr. flight from Istanbul. Already impressed by the unusual geography.

Noticeable presence of solar panels.

Like behemoth skulking creatures these towers appear like an army of soldiers marching towards an indeterminate destination. Each one of a different shape and personality, yet bound together forever. Like family members....

Good example of indigenous adaptive use of natural resources, taking advantage of heat sink qualities of rock and natural ventilation. Geography and geological forms give rise to a particular lifestyle. Isolated dwellings that challenge 'community' — cliff dwellings may do better...

Went on a 90 minute hike through this valley of "fairy chimneys" of every conceivable shape and size, sticking out like fingers pointing to the heavens, or, more earthy subterranean existence giving our world the finger (!).

Dwellings built to and into these towers are well adapted, taking advantage of the soft sandstone-like Cappadocian Rock and the structurally stable shape of the conical ones.

Some are anthropomorphic others phallic, yet others daggerlike weapons of some cosmic war.

23 Dec 2018
Near Göreme in Cappadocia
7:30 am, just in advance of sunrise. Groups of tourists bussed to a staging area for 'breakfast,' then to individual balloons for the rides. Take off and landing spots were different — depending on the wind.

Baskets could hold 16–20 people crammed into well padded pods

Super power fan w/ built-in heating elements

Heavy rubber tire to counterbalance force of fan.

Shivering in 30° chill while the crew prepped massive balloons for lift off. Double fans w/ heaters took about an hr to achieve loft/lift.

From last Saturday's excursion to farmers' market, bedazzled in fresh and bright colored fruit and vegetables, another example of adaptive reuse of a parking garage during the week.

24 Dec '18

Christmas Eve morning in Göreme, after another hike through the 'forests of fairy chimneys,' then settling down to 2nd breakfast at Kelebec (butterfly) Hotel while the rest of the family played Hamami. Amazing adaptive use of these kiva-shaped lava stream protrusions. The Cappadocian Rock is soft tufa, crumbling but retains its structural integrity if undisturbed. Allows one to excavate very efficiently. Quite a number have been 'developed' into single family residences, using solar panels for power.

LanZhou El Makarnasi cut noodles restaurant brought cultural relief to our vacation diet. So much so that we ate there twice despite our deplorable Mandarin.

25 Dec 2018
Christmas Day in Istanbul.

My glass tipped pen from Caroline for Christmas 2018 in Istanbul, with a reservoir that is supposed to last an entire page of text. Supposedly a lifetime guarantee, even for breakage!! Quite an amazing piece of craftsmanship that defies technology and underscores the value of craft and art.

Glass holder and ink well with a 1/16" hole for the nib and cork stopper

25 Dec '18
Leisurely start to Christmas Day in Turkey. It was rainy today and & in the mid 30's, so all manner of winter garb sprung forth before we set off on the day's adventure.

A local breakfast/brunch destination. Great start to Christmas Day activities away from loud Americans and piped Xmas carols.

After a great brunch at Bazlama kahvalti, we walked to Taksim Square to shop for shoes while I observed a rare progress shot of a mosque under construction; quite rare for American architects.

Formed in place concrete alongside delicate dome construction, steel framed dome, lathe and plaster to achieve perfect symmetry.

Taksim Square.

Some family shopping time: first at Caroline's "shoe guy" at Taksim Square, then at random clothing and bowl towel shops on the way to the Galata Tower.

The boys ordered 2 pr. custom Turkish shoes, and we got milk tea and chestnuts for waiting around in the cold.

Upnose view worship the brill of the vault

Went back to Suleimaniye Mosque again with the boys, and was struck by the magnitude of interior space, somewhat disguised by the exterior massing.

Suleimaniye Mosque
26 Dec 2018

Still 26 December...

The obligatory 'tour' of the Grand Bazaar followed lunch of a spicy beans, pickled salad and the ubiquitous bread. Did some serious carpet shopping at Kerimzade with an experienced carpet aficionado Caroline had befriended. Negotiations were a long and drawn out exchange of courteous respect with hard nosed bargaining, all couched in a sort of eastern grace you don't find in the west very often...

e interior, showcasing natural lighting, multi-level and barrels.

Gatehouse to mosque compound.

carpet detail on floor of Süleymaniye Mosque

16'

ENTRANCE DOOR to Süleymaniye mosque for tourists.

Our final stop was the newly renovated Spice Bazaar, where we acquired some beautiful Turkish towels, some Turkish delight and a smattering of miscellaneous souvenirs and spices, including a couple of ounces of Turkish saffron.

59

AT THE END OF THE DAY

*A*s I have invested more time in travel sketching, I have noticed a shift in the way I anticipate and plan for my travels. Aside from the requisite preparation of tools and materials, I find myself preparing my mind to more keenly observe and experience my travels in anticipation that I will be sketching and journaling. This mental and physical preparation seems to turn every journey—even the more mundane trips—into an adventure of discovery and learning.

At the end of the day, travel sketching is like storytelling, and storytelling is at the heart of the human experience. The stories of our lives, in whole or in part, yearned to be told and remembered. They may not be newsworthy to others, but they are entirely meaningful to us as individuals, almost like intangible souvenirs accrued along life's journey.

The procuring of souvenirs might be one of the most enduring traditions—or despised obligations—practiced by travelers around the world for centuries. Overpriced trinkets and tokens purchased from indefatigable hawkers intended to remind us of places we've visited, experiences we've had, and people we've met. Our suitcases often end up becoming bulging repositories of sometimes interesting, largely useless, mementos of our travels.

Since I began travel sketching intentionally, my need or desire for souvenirs - aside from a few obligatory gifts - has diminished significantly. Instead, some of my most prized souvenirs carried back from faraway lands have been my sketches. Long after the

exhilaration of the trip has ebbed, my sketches have become memory triggers, catalysts of meaningful conversation, and treasured keepsakes. Sometimes they evoke a forgotten yet precious memory or emotion that occurred at the time the sketch was made — specific weather conditions, ambient sounds, smells, or tactile sensations.

Travel sketching for me has become integral to the experience and rewards of traveling. My sketchbook and art tools go in my suitcase alongside my toiletry case and phone charger as travel essentials. Not every trip allows me to sketch, but those that do have almost always been more enjoyable and memorable. Nonetheless, while travel sketching remains subordinate to and supportive of the primary objectives of my travels, I am looking forward to when those priorities are reversed, and when my travel plans are made in support of my sketching aspirations.

As of this writing, the world remains in the grip of a ruthless pandemic, and travel restrictions have placed a temporary damper on tourism. However, unlike digital photography which cannot edit a "masked" setting or gain access to restricted venues, travel sketching remains a viable means of conveying the beauty, sights, and sounds of travel experiences by its selective editability limited only by the imagination of the travel artist.

ACKNOWLEDGEMENTS

I am grateful for a great many things in life - family, friends and faith - but in particular for the kind souls who penned such eloquent support for both this book and the craft of drawing by hand - Elaine Adams, Jim Cramer, Ian Fennelly, Justin Gunther, Lai Chee Kien, Timothy Mansfield, John Matteo, Juhani Pallasmaa, Andrew Payne, Angie Plitch, Eny Lee Parker and Sean Stewart. You collectively represent the spectrum of leadership and readership whom I hope will be encouraged to [re]acquaint themselves with the joy and rewards of travel sketching.